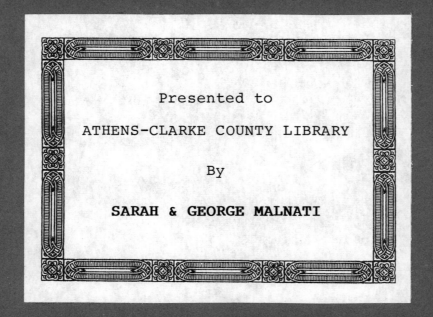

LEARNING HOW TO LEARN

LEARNING HOW TO LEARN

Based on the Works of

L. RON HUBBARD

PUBLICATIONS, INC.

To the Parent or Teacher

Important information about the usage of this book is written on pages 192–194. Familiarity with and application of the data in that section can help your child get more out of the book.

Published by
Bridge Publications, Inc.
4751 Fountain Avenue
Los Angeles, California 90029

ISBN 0-88404-771-7

Printed in the United States of America

Contents

1   Learning How to Learn   1

2   The First Barrier to Study: Lack of Mass   49

3   The Second Barrier to Study: The Skipped Gradient   75

4   The Third and Most Important Barrier to Study: The Misunderstood Word   99

5   Learning the Meanings of Words   131

6   Demonstration and Learning   159

Important Information for Parents and Teachers   192

About the Author   195

For More Information   198

Applied Scholastics Groups and Organizations   199

CHAPTER ONE:

LEARNING HOW TO LEARN

Learning How to Learn

You can learn anything you want to learn!

Learning is not just getting more and more facts.

A fact is something that is known to be true.

Getting more and more facts is not learning.

Learning is understanding new things and getting better ways to do things.

Before you can learn about something you have to want to learn about that thing.

If you think you know all there is to know about something, you will not be able to learn about it.

12

The first thing you have to decide is that you want to learn something.

He wants to learn.

She wants to learn.

Do you want to learn?

Once you have decided that there is something you want to learn, the next thing is to study it.

To *study* means to look at something,

and ask about it,

and read about it,

so you learn about it.

Drill

Use a sheet of paper to write down your answer.

What does *learning* mean?

Drill

Use a sheet of paper to write down your answer.

What does *study* mean?

Drill

Use a sheet of paper to write down your answer.

How could you learn to take care of a pet dog?

Drill

Choose something you want to learn about. Use a sheet of paper to write down how you would learn about that thing.

Why You Study

Many people think that they study so they can pass a test.

But that is not what learning is about.

That is not why you study.

You study to *use* what you have learned.

Drill

Use a sheet of paper to write down your answer.

How will you use what you have learned in this section of this book?

Trouble with Study

Some people do not know how to study, so they have trouble learning.

He does not know how to study.

She does not know how to study.

He does not know how to study.

Sometimes you might run into trouble when you are studying and feel like giving up.

If you understand why you run into trouble and you learn how to handle it, you can study easily.

You can get pretty smart!

This book can help you learn how to learn.

It can teach you how to study.

Drill

Use a sheet of paper to write down your answers.

a. What would you like to learn about?

b. How would it help you to learn about that thing?

Barriers to Study

When you study, you sometimes run into a *barrier* to learning what you want to learn.

A *barrier* is something that blocks the way or stops you from going on.

If you wanted to learn how to sew,

but you had never seen anyone sew,

you might have trouble.

This could be a *barrier* to *study*.

A barrier to study can make
it hard for you to learn anything.

But when you know what the barriers to study are and you can see them and handle them, you do not have to be stopped!

You can learn anything you want to learn!

Drill

Use a sheet of paper to write down your answer.

What is a barrier?

CHAPTER TWO:

THE FIRST BARRIER TO STUDY: LACK OF MASS

The First Barrier to Study: Lack of Mass

The first barrier to study is not having the real thing there that you are studying about.

The real things or the objects
that you study about are called *mass*.

If you were studying about cars, you could get the mass of a car by going to a real car and looking at it and touching it.

If you were reading about animals, you could get the mass of animals by going to a zoo or a farm.

Drill

Use a sheet of paper to write down your answer.

How could you get mass if you were studying about whales?

Studying about something without having the mass of what you are studying can give you trouble. It can make you feel different ways.

It can make you feel squashed.

It can make you feel bent,

sort of spinny,

sort of lifeless,

bored,

or angry.

You can wind up with your stomach feeling funny.

You may get headaches.

You will feel dizzy from time to time

and very often your eyes will hurt.

The way to stop this from happening is to get the mass of what you are studying.

Sometimes you cannot get the real object
you are studying about.

When this happens pictures help. Movies would help too.

But reading books or listening to someone talk does not give you mass.

They do not take the place of what you are studying about.

Drill

Use a sheet of paper to write down your answers.

a. Draw a picture of a person feeling

squashed

bent

spinny

lifeless

bored

angry

b. Why would a student feel these ways?

c. What could you do to help a student who felt these ways?

Drill

Find the mass for each thing listed here and touch it or point to it.

a. water

b. numbers

c. Earth

d. people

e. a light

Drill

Use a sheet of paper to write down your answers.

a. What would you do if you and your brother were in your bedroom and he was explaining to you about the engine in your dad's car and you started to feel bored and your head started to ache?

b. What would you do if your friend was reading a book about how to take care of hamsters but he felt spinny?

CHAPTER THREE:

THE SECOND BARRIER TO STUDY:
THE SKIPPED GRADIENT

The Second Barrier to Study: The Skipped Gradient

A gradient is a way of learning or doing something step by step. A gradient can be easy and each step can be done easily.

Or a gradient can be hard and each step is difficult to do.

You learn how to do something by learning to do each part of it step by step.

You go through the first step and learn how to do it.

Then you go to the next step and learn how to do that.

You learn how to do each step well and then you can do the whole thing.

Learning something step by step
is called learning on a gradient.

If you hit a step that seems too hard to do or you feel you can't understand it, you have skipped a gradient.

"Skipped" means *left out* or *missed.*

If you don't fully understand a step of something you are learning or miss a step, you will have a skipped gradient.

Skipping a gradient is a barrier to study.

If you have skipped a gradient you may feel a sort of confusion or reeling.

"Reeling" means moving or swaying like you might fall.

An example is a person trying to build something.

He is confused and sort of reeling.

There was too much of a jump because he did not understand what he was doing,

and he jumped to the next thing and that step was too steep.

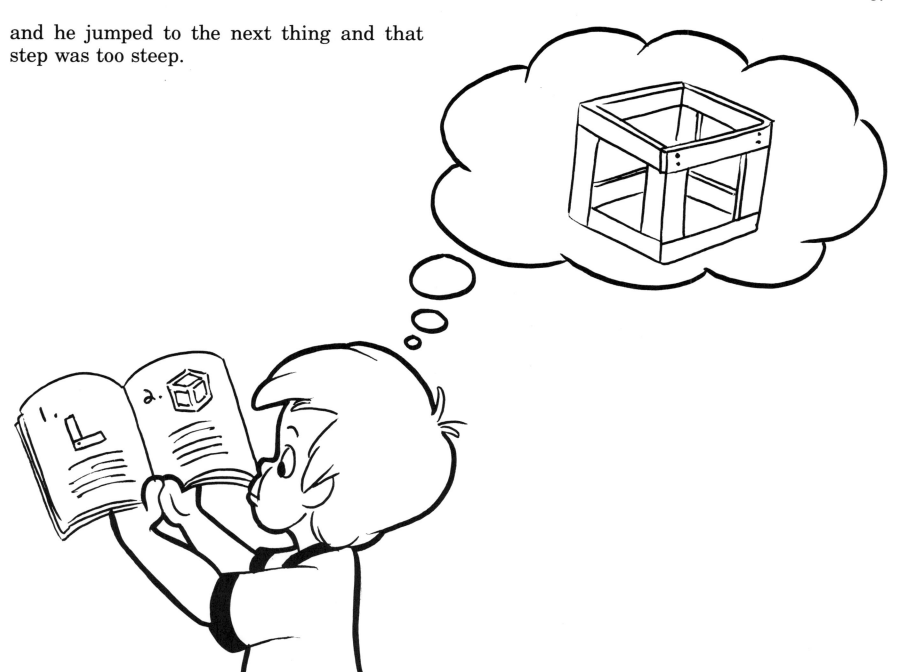

He will think his trouble is with this new step.

But it is not.

His trouble is at the end of the step he thought he understood well.

Find out what he thought he understood well just before he got all confused.

You will find he did not really understand
that step well.

Get this step understood well,

and he will be able to do the next step.

The gradient is no longer skipped.

Drill

Use a sheet of paper to draw a picture of a person who skipped a gradient.

Drill

Use a sheet of paper to write down your answers.

a. Why should you learn new things step by step?

b. What can happen if you do not learn things step by step?

96

Drill

Use a sheet of paper to write down your answers.

a. Think of a time that you learned something step by step.

b. Draw a picture that shows each step that you did.

Drill

Use a sheet of paper to write down your answer.

You are reading a book but you feel very confused about what you are reading. You are also reeling. What should you do?

CHAPTER FOUR:

THE THIRD AND MOST IMPORTANT BARRIER TO STUDY: THE MISUNDERSTOOD WORD

The Third and Most Important Barrier to Study: The Misunderstood Word

The third and most important barrier to study is the *misunderstood word*.

"Mis" means *not* or *wrongly.*

"Misunderstood" means *not understood* or *wrongly understood.*

A misunderstood word is a word which is *not understood,*

or a word which is *wrongly understood.*

She has a misunderstood word.

He has a misunderstood word.

She has a misunderstood word.

He has a misunderstood word.

A misunderstood word
can be a big word

alphabet

or a small word.

him

Have you ever come to the end of a page and realized that you did not remember what you had read?

If you come to the end of a page and do not remember what you have read then there was a word on the page that you did not understand.

Going past a word that you do not understand can make you feel blank,

or tired,

or like you are not there.

You might also feel worried or upset.

This does not happen only when you are reading.

This can also happen when you hear a word you do not understand.

The only reason a person would stop studying or get confused or not be able to learn is because he has passed a word that he did not understand.

A misunderstood word can make you seem silly.

It can stop you from doing the things you
are studying about.

It can make you want to stop studying.

The way to handle this barrier is to look earlier in what you were reading for a misunderstood word.

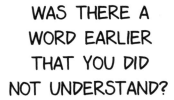

Go back to before you got into trouble,

find the misunderstood word

and look it up in a dictionary.

A dictionary is a word book. A dictionary contains the meanings of words and other information about them. A dictionary can be used to find out what a word means, how to say a word, how to spell a word, how to use a word and many other things about words.

Symbols can be misunderstood in the same way that words can be misunderstood.

A symbol is a mark or sign that means something.

Symbols also need to be understood.

The misunderstood word is the most important of the barriers to study because it is the one that can stop you from learning anything at all.

So if you are feeling blank,

or tired,

or not there,

or worried and upset while you are studying,

it is *always*
because of a misunderstood
word or symbol.

Drill

Use a sheet of paper to draw a picture of a person feeling

a. blank

b. tired

c. not there

d. worried and upset

Drill

Use a sheet of paper to write down your answers.

a. Why would a person feel blank or tired or not there while he was studying?

b. If a person felt blank or tired or not there while he was studying, what could you do to help him?

Drill

Use a sheet of paper to write down your answer.

You are reading a book at home. You get to the bottom of the page but you do not remember what the page was about. Why would this happen?

CHAPTER FIVE:

LEARNING THE MEANINGS OF WORDS

Learning the Meanings of Words

If you are studying and do not feel as bright as you did,

or if you are taking too long on what you are studying,

or you are yawning,

or doodling,

or daydreaming,

you have gone past a misunderstood word.

If you have a misunderstood word, then there are some steps you need to do.

1. Look earlier in your book and find the word you do not understand.

2. Find the word in a dictionary.

3. Look over all of the definitions and find the definition that fits in what you were reading.

A definition is a statement of the meaning of a word.

4. Read the definition that fits.

5. Make up sentences using the word that way until you really understand that definition of the word.

This might take many sentences. Maybe ten or more.

That is okay.

The important thing is that you understand what the word means.

THE INK SPILLED ON THE LEG OF HIS PANTS.

HE TORE THE LEG OF HIS PANTS ON A FENCE.

THE LEG OF HIS PANTS WAS TOO SHORT.

6. When you understand the definition that fits in what you were reading, then learn each of the other definitions the same way.

leg ONE OF THE BODY PARTS ON WHICH HUMANS AND ANIMALS SUPPORT THEMSELVES AND WALK.

7. After you learn all of the definitions of that word then go back to what you were reading. If you are not bright and ready to study again, then there is still another word that you do not understand.

Do steps 1–7 again until you are bright and ready to study again.

8. Then start studying from the place where the misunderstood word was.

(If there was more than one misunderstood word, start studying again from where the earliest misunderstood you found was.)

More About Learning New Words

Sometimes words are used together to make a different meaning than the words have when used by themselves.

For example, here is a sentence: "The actor's performance will bring the house down." "Bring the house down" means "to receive very loud applause." It does not mean that the actor is going to lower a house using a crane. When words are used like this it is called an *idiom*.

"Bring the house down" does not mean this:

"Bring the house down" means this:

Have you ever heard anyone say, "Let's shake a leg"?

"Shake a leg" does *not* mean that you should shake your leg.

"Shake a leg" means "to dance."

"Shake a leg" can also mean "to hurry."

Dictionaries give the idioms of a word after the definitions of a word.

If you are learning a word that has idioms you should learn the idioms after the other definitions of the word.

Use the idioms in sentences just like you do when you are learning the other definitions of a word.

When you are learning a word, you may find a word in the definition that you do not understand.

Find that word in the dictionary too, and learn all of its definitions.

Then go back to the first word you were learning.

When you understand all the words in what you are studying you can understand the whole thing.

A MOUSE IS A NICE PET.

THE MOUSE SCARED HER.

MOUSE 1. A SMALL GNAWING ANIMAL THAT LIVES IN HOUSES AND FIELDS.

Drill

Find the word "chicken" in a dictionary. Show another person how you would learn what the word "chicken" means by doing the steps of how to learn the meaning of a word.

Drill

Find a word in something you are studying that you do not know the meaning of. Use a dictionary to find out what that word means using the eight steps of how to learn the meaning of a word.

CHAPTER SIX:

DEMONSTRATION AND LEARNING

Demonstration and Learning

The word "demonstrate" means to show, or to show how something works. A *demonstration* is something done to show something or how it works.

Doing a demonstration is a good way to teach someone something. Demonstration is an important part of learning.

When you are studying, you can do a "demonstration" or "demo" with a "demo kit." A demo kit is made of different objects such as corks, caps, paper clips, pen tops, rubber bands or other similar objects. You can demonstrate an idea or rule or anything you are studying with your hands and the pieces of your demo kit.

This is a demo kit.

If you ran into something you could not figure out, a demo kit would help you to understand it. You can make different pieces of the demo kit represent the objects you are studying about. You can move the objects around to see how something works.

By doing this you are getting mass to go along with the ideas you study.

164

HE SEES A BIKE, WHICH IS
THIS PAPER CLIP, AND LOOKS
AT ALL THE PARTS OF THE BIKE.
THEN HE HAS THE MASS
OF WHAT HE IS STUDYING.

Drill

Make a demo kit for yourself.

Drill

Using your demo kit, show another person how you would get from home to school.

Drill

Using your demo kit, demo the first barrier to study to another person.

Demo how you would help someone who has the first barrier to study.

Drill

Using your demo kit, demo the second barrier to study to another person.

Demo how you would help someone who has the second barrier to study.

Drill

Using your demo kit, demo the third barrier to study to another person.

Demo how you would help someone who has the third barrier to study.

Drill

Use a sheet of paper to write down your answer.

Why would you do a demo when you are studying?

Clay Demonstration

Another way to demonstrate what you are studying is to make it in clay. Demonstrating something in clay can help you to figure out how something is put together, how it looks or how it works. It can help you understand better what you are studying.

If you come across something you cannot figure out, you can work it out in clay.

There are many ways that clay can be used.

People who design new cars make clay
models of cars to see how they will look.

A general will make a model of the battle-field so he can get an idea of how to win the battle.

You can understand *anything* better by demonstrating it in clay. Say you wanted to figure out how to organize your room better so you could fit a new desk in it. You could make a model of the room and the furniture and other things. Then you could move them around and find the best way to arrange them.

How to Do a Clay Demo

Clay demos are done using clay to make the mass of the thing. Then a label is made to say what the thing is. Let's see how this works.

Say you wanted to do a clay demo of a pencil. First, make a thin roll of clay. This is the pencil lead. You would make a label using paper and a pen that said "LEAD" and stick it on the thin roll of clay.

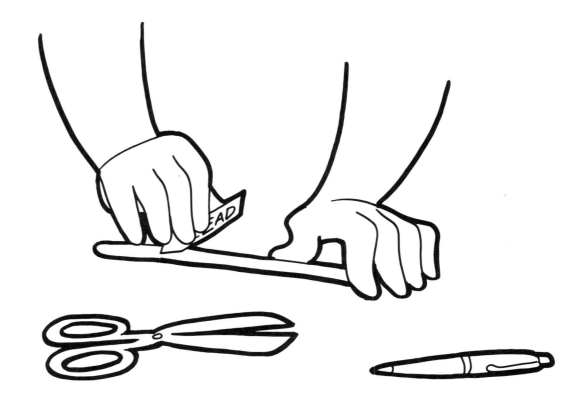

Next, put another layer of clay with the thin roll sticking out a little bit at one end. This is the wood part of the pencil, so you would make a label that said "WOOD" and stick it on.

Then put another little piece of clay on the end. This is the rubber eraser, so you would label it "RUBBER" and stick it on that piece of clay.

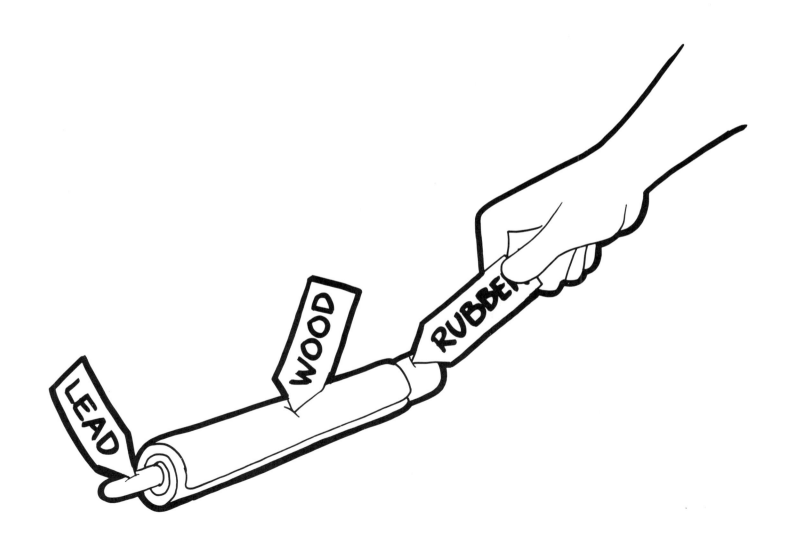

Finally, you make a label for the whole thing. This label says "PENCIL."

Clay demos must be large. If a clay demo is too small it might not make what you are studying real enough. Making the things you are studying in clay can help make them more *real* to you.

His clay demo is large.

Her clay demo is too small.

Making BIG clay demos works better to help you understand what you are studying.

Even a thought can be shown in clay. You can use a thin ring of clay to show a thought or idea. Here is a clay demo of a person thinking about a ball.

If you don't understand something in life you can work it out in clay and understand it better. *Anything* can be shown in clay.

Clay demos are an important part of learning how to learn.

Sketching

A sketch is a rough drawing of something.

Sketching is also a part of demonstration and part of working things out.

GO TO THE CORNER, TURN RIGHT, GO TO THE END OF THE STREET, THEN YOU ARE AT MY HOUSE.

OKAY!

You sometimes see people doing sketching at work. They work things out for themselves by sketching it.

Drill

Do a sketch of how to get from your house to your friend's house.

Summary

People who do well in life never really stop studying and learning.

There are a lot of things to learn.

Learning is not hard to do and it can be fun.

Now that you know the barriers to study and how to handle them, you can learn anything you want to learn.

And you can help others learn too!

WE ARE GOING TO FIND THE WORD YOU DO NOT UNDERSTAND.

Drill

Use a sheet of paper to write down your answer.

Why will it help you to know how to study?

Drill

Get a short, simple book about something you are interested in learning.

Read the book. If you run into any of the barriers to study while you are reading, then use what you have learned in this book to handle the barriers.

Use a sheet of paper to write down what you did.

CONGRATULATIONS!

You have completed *Learning How to Learn.*

Knowing how to learn is a valuable skill and it is very well done that you have learned this.

Have fun applying your new skills to anything you study. That is what they are for!

Important Information for Parents and Teachers

This book has been published to fill an important need.

We live now in an instruction-book world. Our civilization is highly technical.

Formal education today goes into one's twenties, nearly a third of a lifetime. But what happens when a person leaves school? Can he *do* what he studied? And factually, education begins *before* a person learns to speak and continues throughout his entire life. Can he *do* what he has studied outside of the classrooms of his school days?

Any child's future success and happiness are dependent on his ability to learn. Innately, this ability is very strong. Children possess an almost boundless fascination about everything in life. A curiosity and eagerness to explore and learn is turned on "high" at a very young age.

Children are confronted with so many things they don't yet understand. They have been told that learning is the key to their future. But it is a mean trick to tell someone that he must learn and then not teach him HOW to learn.

Learning How to Learn contains fundamental principles of L. Ron Hubbard's researches into the field of education, where he isolated the basics which underlie all forms of learning. His breakthroughs resulted in Study Technology, the first subject which actually deals with HOW to learn. Study Technology is basic to any specific subject since it deals with learning itself, the barriers to learning and remedies for these barriers.

Learning How to Learn presents the fundamentals of Study Technology at a level that a child can assimilate, understand and *use*. It is a breakthrough in the field of learning and education for preteenagers and teenagers.

Using the Book for Maximum Benefit

Reading Level

The book is written so that a child can study it by himself. It has been written for children eight through twelve, though children as young as six have successfully read the book, grasped the concepts and put them to use.

Drills

There are drills throughout the book which get the child to *apply* what he has read. These are key to gaining the most from the book and the child should be encouraged to do them thoroughly.

Familiarity

In working with a son or daughter on the book or in using it in a classroom, it will help if you have read the book first and are familiar with its contents. Though simply written, the data presented here are not to be found in any previously published book on education or learning. The concepts are totally original with the researches of L. Ron Hubbard into the field of education and his discoveries on the mental phenomena which block learning, the physiological manifestations which result from these blocks and the specific remedies for each one.

Ensuring Understanding

In giving this book to your son or daughter and in working with him or her on the book or in using it in a classroom situation, there is one very important datum about study of which you should be aware:

THE ONLY REASON A PERSON GIVES UP A STUDY OR BECOMES CONFUSED OR UNABLE TO LEARN IS BECAUSE HE HAS GONE PAST A WORD THAT WAS NOT UNDERSTOOD.

The confusion or inability to grasp or learn comes AFTER a word that the person did not have defined and understood.

Have you ever had the experience of coming to the end of a page and realizing you didn't know what you had read? Well, somewhere earlier on that page you went past a word that you had no definition for or an incorrect definition for.

Here's an example. "It was found that when the crepuscule arrived the children were quieter and when it was not present, they were livelier." You see what happens. You think you don't understand the whole idea, but the inability to understand came entirely from the one word you could not define, *crepuscule,* which means twilight or darkness.

The datum about not going past an undefined word is the most important datum in study and is thoroughly covered in the book on pages 101–127. Every subject a person has taken up and then abandoned or done poorly at had its words which the person failed to get defined. It is the most important barrier to study and a parent or teacher should be familiar with this datum. The phenomena which occur after a person has unknowingly encountered a word he or she did not understand are quite distinct and easily recognized once you know what you are looking at.

As simple as it seems, many of the tribulations in children's lives can often be traced back to words they have not understood in their reading materials or in life.

Use as a Reference Book

After a child has read the book and learned these study skills, he can and should be referred back to his materials whenever necessary during his future studies. As startling as it may seem, a workable technology of how to study something was foreign to the field of education before L. Ron Hubbard's researches in the area. *Learning How to Learn* can be used time and time again as a reminder of the basics of successful learning.

Further Information

Numerous schools across the United States and throughout Europe now utilize Mr. Hubbard's study technology to promote faster learning with increased comprehension.

If you or your child or student encounter any difficulties in reading or applying the data in this book there are addresses of schools and institutions on the following pages you can contact. These organizations make exclusive use of Study Technology and will be happy to provide any assistance needed as well as provide further information about these new advances in education.

There is also a toll-free number you can call for assistance or for further information: (1-800-424-5397).

When a child knows how to gain more knowledge, his enthusiasm for learning will never become stale. The basic concepts presented in this book apply to anyone, not just children. Once a child grasps the tools contained here these will become a natural part of his approach to living and he will use them throughout all his activities in life.

The fundamentals contained in *Learning How to Learn* are sweeping discoveries in the field of education and they open the gates to learning and application.

When a child has learned how to learn, all knowledge becomes available to him, assuring that, whatever his fields of interest, he will have the greatest possible chance for fulfillment and success.

About the Author

L. Ron Hubbard was no stranger to education. Although his main profession was that of a professional writer, in a long, event-filled and productive life he spent thousands of hours researching in the education field, lecturing and teaching.

He was born in Tilden, Nebraska on 13 March 1911, and his early years were spent on his grandfather's ranch in the wilds of Montana. As the son of a US Navy commander, he was well on the way to becoming a seasoned traveler by the age of eight, and by the time he was nineteen he had logged over a quarter of a million miles.

He enrolled in George Washington University in 1930, taking classes in mathematics and engineering. But his was not a quiet academic life. He took up flying in the pioneer days of aviation, learning to pilot first glider planes and then powered aircraft. He worked as a freelance reporter and photographer. He directed expeditions to the Caribbean and Puerto Rico, and later, to Alaska. The world was his classroom and he studied voraciously, gathering experience which provided the background for his later writings, research and discoveries.

Some of his first published articles were nonfiction, based upon his aviation experience. Soon he began to draw from his travels to produce a wide variety of fiction stories and novels: adventure, mystery, westerns, fantasy and science fiction.

The proceeds from his fiction writing funded his main line of research and exploration—how to improve the human condition. His nonfiction works cover such diverse subjects as drug rehabilitation, marriage and family, success at work, statistical analysis, public relations, art, marketing and much, much more. But he did more than write books—he also delivered over 6,000 lectures and conducted courses to impart his own discoveries to others.

However, in order to learn, one must be able to read and understand. Therefore, L. Ron Hubbard tackled the problem of teaching others how to study. His research uncovered the basic reason for the failure of a student to grasp any subject. He discovered the barriers to full comprehension of what one is studying, and developed methods by which anyone can improve his ability to learn and to *apply* the data that he is being taught. He wrote a considerable body of work on this subject, which he termed *study technology.*

L. Ron Hubbard's advanced technology of study is now used by an estimated two million students and thousands of teachers in universities and school systems internationally. His educational materials have been translated into twelve languages to meet this worldwide demand for the first truly *workable* technology of how to study. Organizations delivering L. Ron Hubbard's study technology have been established in the United States, Australia, South Africa, Canada, Austria, Great Britain, Pakistan, Mexico, Germany, Denmark, France, Italy, Venezuela and China.

L. Ron Hubbard departed his body on 24 January 1986. His contributions to the world of education have meant new hope, better understanding and increased ability for millions of students and educators the world over.

Additional Books for Students by L. Ron Hubbard

Study Skills for Life • Written for preteens and young teenagers, this book teaches students how to *use* what they are studying so they can attain the goals they set for themselves. Using these skills, they can break the barriers to learning.

How to Use a Dictionary Picture Book for Children • One of the ingredients of a quality education is giving a student the tools he needs to study successfully on his own. No matter the subject or field being learned, one has to know how to use the dictionary to clearly understand the meaning of words. This book contains the secret of how to put education into action.

Grammar and Communication • The ability to communicate is vital to happiness and self-confidence. But getting one's communication across is dependent upon being able to speak and write correctly. The unique approach to grammar taught in this book can open the world of words to a child—granting him the strong sense of self-esteem which results from the ability to read well, write clearly and communicate effectively.

When children can learn and think for themselves, the world is an open book.

TO ORDER THESE BOOKS OR TO GET MORE INFORMATION ON L. RON HUBBARD'S STUDY TECHNOLOGY, CALL: 1-800-424-5397

For more information on educational books and materials by L. Ron Hubbard, contact your nearest distributor:

Association for Better Living
  and Education International
6331 Hollywood Blvd., Suite 700
Los Angeles, California 90028

Association for Better Living
  and Education Canada
696 Yonge Street
Toronto, Ontario, Canada
M4Y 2A7

Association for Better Living
  and Education East US
349 W. 48th Street
New York, NY 10036

Association for Better Living
  and Education Europe
Sankt Nikolaj Vej 4–6
Frederiksberg C
1953 Copenhagen
Denmark

Instituto de Tecnologia para la
  Educacion A.C.
Tetla #6
Colonia Ruiz Cortines
Delegación Coyoacán
C.P. 64630 México D.F.

Association for Better Living
  and Education United Kingdom
Saint Hill Manor
East Grinstead, W. Sussex
England RH19 4JY

Association for Better Living
  and Education Australia,
  New Zealand and Oceania
201 Castlereagh Street
Sydney, New South Wales 2000
Australia

Association for Better Living
  and Education Africa
Security Building, 4th Floor
95 Commissioner Street
Johannesburg 2001, South Africa

Association for Better Living
  and Education Italy
Via Nerino, 8
20213 Milan, Italy

Association for Better Living
  and Education Russia
48 Vavilova Street
Building 4, Suite 169
Moscow 117333, Russia

You can also contact any of the groups and organizations on the following pages which use L. Ron Hubbard's study technology.

Applied Scholastics Groups and Organizations

Applied Scholastics International
7060 Hollywood Blvd., Suite 200
Los Angeles, California 90028

United States of America

California

Ability Academy
PO Box 601091
San Diego, California 92160

Ability Plus School—La Canada
4490 Cornishon Ave.
La Canada, California 91011

Ability Plus School—Orange
County
333 S. Prospect
Orange, California 92669

Ability Plus School—Woodland
Hills
Dept. 503, PO Box 4172
Woodland Hills, California 91365

Academy for Smart Kids
4632 Russell Ave.
Los Angeles, California 90027

Applied Scholastics—Crescenta
Valley
7944 Day Street
Sunland, California 91040

Applied Scholastics—Los Angeles
503 Central Ave.
Glendale, California 91203

Applied Scholastics—San Francisco
39355 California St. #107
Fremont, California 94538

Applied Scholastics
South Orange County
6 Heritage
Irvine, California 92714

California Ranch School
17305 Santa Rosa Mine Road
Gavilan Hills, California 92370

Carroll-Rees Academy
4474 De Longpre
Los Angeles, California 90027

Delphi Academy—Los Angeles
4490 Cornishon Ave.
La Canada, California 91011

Delphi Academy—Sacramento
5325 Engle Rd. #600
Carmichael, California 95608

Delphi Academy—San Francisco
445 E. Charleston Rd. #7
Palo Alto, California 94306

Élan Esprit
1860 Villa St.
Mountain View, California 96043

Expansion Consultants, Inc.
550 N. Brand Street 700
Glendale, California 91203

Golden Gate Apple School
379 Colusa Ave.
Kensington, California 94707

Karen Aranas Tutoring Center
933 Edwards Ave. #24
Santa Rosa, California 95401

Learning Connection
2528 Canyon Dr.
Hollywood, California 90068

Legacy Learning Group
2789 Cornelius Drive
San Pablo, California 94806

Lewis Carroll Academy of the Arts
5425 Cahuenga Blvd.
N. Hollywood, California 91601

Los Gatos Academy
220 Belgatos Road
Los Gatos, California 95032

Mojave Desert School
44579 Temescal
Newberry Springs, California 92365

Pinewood Academy
4490 Cornishon Ave.
La Canada, California 91011

Real School
50 El Camino
Corte Madera, California 94925

Smart Apple Tutoring Service
1310 Chuckwagon Dr.
Sacramento, California 95834

The Tutoring School
3250 Fairesta St. #A-7
La Crescenta, California 91214

Colorado

Applied Scholastics—Colorado
3958 S. Kalamath
Englewood, Colorado 80112

Connecticut

Ability Plus Connecticut
PO Box 19
Cheshire, Connecticut 06410

Standard Education
3 David Drive
Simsbury, Connecticut 06070

Florida

Astra
615 Oak Ave. #6
Clearwater, Florida 34616

A To Be School, Inc.
531 Franklin Street
Clearwater, Florida 34616

Jefferson Academy, Inc.
1301 N. Highland Ave.
Clearwater, Florida 34615

Renaissance Academy
1301 N. Highland Ave.
Clearwater, Florida 34615

Studema International
PO Box 10559
Clearwater, Florida 34617

TRUE School, Inc.
1831 Drew Street
Clearwater, Florida 34625

Georgia

Lafayette Academy
2417 Canton Road
Marietta, Georgia 30066

Illinois

The Learning School, Inc.
864 E. Northwest Hwy.
Mount Prospect, Illinois 60056

Louisiana

Applied Scholastics Lafayette
210 Elmwood
Lafayette, Louisiana 70503

Massachusetts

Delphi Academy—Boston
564 Blue Hill Ave.
Milton, Massachusetts 02186

Michigan

Cedars Center
1602 W. 3rd Ave.
Flint, Michigan 48504

Recording Institute of Detroit, Inc.
14611 E. Nine Mile Road
East Detroit, Michigan 48021

Minnesota

Beacon Heights Academy
12325 Highway 55
Plymouth, Minnesota 55441

Missouri

Ability School—St. Louis
14298 Olive St. Road
St. Louis, Missouri 63017

New Hampshire

Bear Hill School, Inc.
PO Box 417
Pittsfield, New Hampshire 03263

New Jersey
Ability School—New Jersey
192 W. Demarest Ave.
Englewood, New Jersey 07631

Oregon
Columbia Academy, Inc.
1808 SE Belmont
Portland, Oregon 97214

The Delphian School—Oregon
20950 SW Rock Creek Road
Sheridan, Oregon 97378

Eagle Oak School
PO Box 12
Bridal Veil, Oregon 97010

Pennsylvania
Applied Scholastics Pennsylvania
PO Box 662
Reading, Pennsylvania 19603

Texas
Austin Academy of Higher
   Learning
10503 Robinwood Circle
Austin, Texas 78753

Perfect Schooling, Inc.
402 Town and Country Village
Houston, Texas 77024

Utah
Ability School—Utah
913 E. Syrena Circle
Sandy, Utah 89094

Virginia
Chesapeake Ability School
5533 Industrial Dr.
Springfield, Virginia 22151

Washington
Washington Academy of Knowledge
5801 Phinney Ave. N. #402
Seattle, Washington 98101

Wyoming
Great American Ski School
PO Box 427
Jackson, Wyoming 83001

Canada
Académie Phénix
9222 Chateaubriand
Montreal, Québec 42M 1X8
Canada

Applied Scholastics
   (National Office)
840 Pape Ave., Suite 209
Toronto, Ontario M4K 3T6
Canada

Education Alive—Halifax
2130 Armcrescent West
Halifax, Nova Scotia B3L 3E3
Canada

Education Alive—Kentville
27 James Street
Kentville, Nova Scotia B4N 2A1
Canada

Education Alive—Toronto
840 Pape Ave., Suite 201
Toronto, Ontario M4K 3T6
Canada

Effective Education School
8610 Ash Street
Vancouver, British Columbia
   V6P 3M2
Canada

Progressive Academy
12245 131st Street
Edmonton, Alberta T5L 1M8
Canada

Toronto Ability School
85 41st Street
Etobicoke, Ontario M8W 3P1
Canada

Wise Owl Tutoring
342 Blackthorn Ave.
Toronto, Ontario M6N 3J3
Canada

United Kingdom
Effective Education Association
   East Grinstead
31A High Street
East Grinstead, W. Sussex
   RH19 3AF
England

Effective Education Association
   London
2C Falkland Rd.
Kentish Town, London NW5
England

Effective Education Association
   Scotland
31 St. Katharine's Brae
Liberton, Edinburgh EH16 6PY
Scotland

Effective Education Association
   Sunderland
9 Catherine Terrace
Newkyo, Stanley, Co. Durham
   DH9 7TP
England

Greenfields School
Priory Road—Forest Row
E. Sussex RH18 53D
England

Austria
Kreativ College
Rienosslgasse 12
1040 Wien, Austria

Belgium
Brussels Ability School
Rue Auguste Lambiotte 23
1030 Bruxelles
Belgium

Denmark
Amager International School
5th Floor, Graekenlandsvej 51-53
2300 Copenhagen S, Denmark

Applied Scholastics (European
   Office)
F. F. Ulriksgade 13
2100 Copenhagen O, Denmark

Applied Scholastics—Denmark
F. F. Ulriksgade 13
2100 Copenhagen O, Denmark

Foreningen for Effektiv
   Grunduddannelse Aarhus
Hammervaenget 22
8310 Tranbjerg, Denmark

Foreningen for Effektiv
   Grunduddannelse Amager
Graekenlandsvej 53
2300 Copenhagen S, Denmark

Foreningen for Effektiv
   Grunduddannelse Birkerod
Kongevejen 110 B
3460 Birkerod, Denmark

Foreningen for Effektiv
   Grunduddannelse Brondby
   Strand
Hyttebovej 20
2660 Brondby Strand, Denmark

Foreningen for Effektiv
   Grunduddannelse Bronshoj
Klintevej 40
2700 Bronshoj, Denmark

Foreningen for Effektiv
   Grunduddannelse Dania
Daniavej 60 Assens
9550 Mariager, Denmark

Foreningen for Effektiv
   Grunduddannelse Dania
   Erhvervscenter
Daniavej 60 Assens
9550 Mariager, Denmark

Foreningen for Effektiv
   Grunduddannelse Glostrup
Falkevej 20
2600 Glostrup, Denmark

Foreningen for Effektiv
   Grunduddannelse Grinsted
Gronlandsvej 2
7290 Grinsted, Denmark

Foreningen for Effektiv
   Grunduddannelse Hvidovre
Hvidovre Alle 17
2650 Hvidovre, Denmark

Foreningen for Effektiv
   Grunduddannelse Kalundborg
Dalsvinget 5
4400 Kalundborg, Denmark

Foreningen for Effektiv
Grunduddannelse Koge
Straedet 6
Stroby Egede
4600 Koge, Denmark

Foreningen for Effektiv
Grunduddannelse Naestved
H. C. Lumbyesvej 102
4700 Naestved, Denmark

Foreningen for Effektiv
Grunduddannelse Norrebro
Ravnsborggade 6, 5
2200 Copenhagen N, Denmark

Foreningen for Effektiv
Grunduddannelse Norre Sundby
Jorgenbertelsvej 17 A, 1tv
9400 Norre Sundby, Denmark

Foreningen for Effektiv
Grunduddannelse Olstykke
Sajisnej 21
3650 Olstykke, Denmark

Foreningen for Effektiv
Grunduddannelse Osterbro
F. F. Ulriksgade 13
2100 Copenhagen O, Denmark

Foreningen for Effektiv
Grunduddannelse Risskov
Flintebakken 60
8240 Risskov, Denmark

Foreningen for Effektiv
Grunduddannelse Silkeborg
Chr. D. 8. vej 12.1
8600 Silkeborg, Denmark

Foreningen for Effektiv
Grunduddannelse Slagelse
Sct. Mikkelsgade 23
4200 Slagelse, Denmark

Foreningen for Effektiv
Grunduddannelse Tastrup
Kogevej 11
2630 Tastrup, Denmark

Foreningen for Effektiv
Grunduddannelse Vadum
Ulrik Burihovej 69
9430 Vadum, Denmark

Foreningen for Effektiv
Grunduddannelse Vojens
Skovvej 18
6500 Vojens, Denmark

Kildeskolen
Roskildevej 158
2500 Valby, Denmark

France
Applied Scholastics France
49 rue Général de Gaulle
22400 Lamballe
France

Ecole de l'éveil
11 passage Courtois
75011 Paris, France

Irene Chartry Tutoring Service
27 rue Andre Cayron
92600 Asnieres, France

Le Cours pour apprendre
16 rue du Bac
75007 Paris, France

Management Distribution
43 rue Volney
49000 Angers, France

Germany
Applied Scholastics—Germany
Unter Buschweg 118
5000 Köln, Germany

Applied Scholastics Aidlingen
Blumenstrasse 14
7042 Aidlingen
Germany

Applied Scholastics Augsburg
Stettenstrasse 36
8900 Augsburg
Germany

Applied Scholastics Cologne
Unter Buschweg 118
5000 Köln, Germany

Applied Scholastics Düsseldorf
Kruppstrasse 45
4000 Düsseldorf 1
Germany

Applied Scholastics Eisingen
Waldpark 2
7531 Eisingen
Germany

Applied Scholastics Euskirchen
Ringelstrasse 14
5350 Euskirchen-Billig
Germany

Applied Scholastics Hamburg
Swartenhorst 50
2000 Hamburg 71
Germany

Applied Scholastics Hünfelden
Obergasse 1
6257 Hünfelden-Ohren
Germany

Applied Scholastics Munich 1
Wildalpjochstr. 10
8000 München 82
Germany

Applied Scholastics Munich 2
Bluten Str. 16
8000 München 40
Germany

Applied Scholastics Pocking
Feichtetstr. 41
8134 Pocking
Germany

Applied Scholastics Velbert
Am Neuhanskothen 51
5620 Velbert 11
Germany

Holland
Lafayette School
Kastanjelaan 15
1394 CB Nederhorst den Berg
Holland

Italy
Associazione Studio Moderno
Piazza Cittadella, 13
41100 Modena, Italy

Russia
Center Team
Panfiorova St.
117261 Moscow
Russia

Education Center Siberia
Ussolye—Sibirshoye, 66547
Kuibysheva Str. 1a
Trkutsh Region
Russia

Sweden
Applied Scholastics—Sweden
Terrängvägen 39
126 61 Hägersten, Sweden

Daghemmet U-Care
Grusåsgränd 88
122 49 Enskede, Sweden

Fritidshemmet Robin Hood
Terrängvägen 39
126 61 Hägersten, Sweden

Måsens daghem
Tuppgrand 10-14
122 50 Enskede, Sweden

Solrosen
Örtugsgatan 13
414 79 Göteborg
Sweden

Studema-Skolan
Terrängvägen 39
126 61 Hägersten, Sweden

Switzerland
Verein ZIEL
Postfach 5114
6002 Luzern, Switzerland

Australia
Ability Plus
32 Ryan St.
Northcote Victoria 3070
Australia

Applied Scholastics ANZO
319 Canterbury Road
Ringwood, Victoria 3134
Australia

Applied Scholastics Training Centre
#404, 3 Smail St.
Broadway NSW 2007
Australia

The Athena School
697 Princes Hwy.
Tempe, NSW 2044
Australia

Jenny Gellie Tutoring Services
21 Railway Parade
Hazelbrook NSW 2779
Australia

Yarralinda School
319 Canterbury Road
Ringwood, Victoria 3134
Australia

Japan
Applied Scholastics Japan
3-13-36E 1001
Kusunoki-cho, Nishi-Ku
Hiroshima
Japan 733

Malaysia
Applied Scholastics Institute
No. 42-2A, Jalan Tun
   Sambanthan 3
50470 Kuala Lumpur
Malaysia

Pakistan
Effective Education Association—
   Karachi
348 CP Berar Society, Block 7/8
Dhoraji Colony
Karachi-5, Pakistan

Africa
A+ School
28 Church Street
Halfway House
Pretoria 1685, South Africa

Education Alive—Cape Town
51 Station Road
Observatory
Cape Town 7925, South Africa

Education Alive—Johannesburg
3rd Floor CDH House
217 Jeppe Street
Johannesburg 2001, South Africa

Education Alive (National Office)
3rd Floor CDH House
217 Jeppe Street
Johannesburg 2001, South Africa

Greenfields Education Complex
PO Box 346
Buea SWP
Cameroon, Africa

Latin America

Colombia
Instituto de Ayuda Escolar
Cra 28 No. 91-39
Sante Fe de Bogotá
Colombia

Mexico
Educacion Del Mañana
Cordobanes 47
Col. San Jose Insurgentes
03900 México D.F.

Grupo Iniciativa
Calzada de Tlalpan #934
Col. Nativitas
03500 México D.F.

ITE de México (National Office)
Tetla #6 Col. Ruiz Cortines
Delegación Coyoacán
C.P. 04630 México D.F.

ITE de Guadalajara
Jazmin 376 S.R.
Guadalajara, Jalisco
México

ITE de Jalapa
Corregidora #24-A
Col. Centro
Jalapa, Veracruz
México